Catfish and After

Gene Hult

Brighten Press

Houston

2019

Copyright © 2019 by Gene Hult

All rights reserved. This book or any portion thereof may not be reproduced or used in any manner or media whatsoever without the permission of the publisher or author except for the use of brief quotations in a book review or academic essay.

First Edition, 2019

ISBN 978-1-7335380-1-5 (ebook)
ISBN 978-1-7335380-0-8 (paperback)

Brighten Press
Houston, Texas

info@brightenpress.com
www.brightenpress.com

Cover image manipulated from a drawing by Léonard Baldner, 1666.

"Seizure" first appeared in *You Can Hear the Ocean: An Anthology of Classic and Current Poetry*.

"Gifts" first appeared in the anthology *A Few More Winter Tales*.

Catfish and After

Contents

Catfish — 1
After — 33

- Supplies — 35
- Brood — 38
- Gracious — 40
- Laurel — 45
- Western — 48
- Nothing — 50
- Iterate — 52
- Hike — 57
- Merge — 59
- Nineteen — 61
- Seizure — 63
- Closer — 69
- Omen — 71
- Scratch — 73

Hard	76
Shelter	78
Bandy	81
Bronzed	83
Drift	86
Best	88
Motion	90
Exurb	92
Sophist	96
Privy	98
Knoll	100
Gifts	102
Coast	108
About the Author	110

Catfish

for Colin

Let him have his secrets.

Glimpsed release from solitude
constricted by jealousy's petty tang,
accounting for grinding seconds
we remain unmet.

Even no phone number
or last name, I trust
in genuine self-protection
for listening laughter.

Deflection shudders greed
of possession, parity of imaginary
slights, disconnection distraction.

Gagging on magnitude,
what I would lose.

Message me when you're home.

What are you, deaf?

What will you wear
on our first date,
a wifebeater?

How hoary, vexed by text,
in query suspension; communication
otherwise easy, extraordinary.

All unconfirmed,
alternative earworms.

Midtown architect,
industrial fraternity
bluster and muscle, but mute
by prideful declaration.

Goateed and too tall,
deprecatingly depressive,
enticingly negative,
photos of physical exuberance
with bristled beauty,

believably introverted
in knockabout silence.

Clean cobwebs, decals
of no confidence molder
in cold storage.

More barred
increases invasivity.

Only impertinent asks
add echoes of ulterior motives
should've slid as snuck subtext.

Tease me as you agree.

Refusal may imply betrayal
on boundaries of kind,
imposing permissible
to shelter in muddy eddy.

Coughing skinniness
tinged with stifled acids.

You enjoy me,
so let's meet,
expose yourself
to my thirst.

I exceed interest
in your difference.

Inoperable fused cochlea
complements my misophonia.

Honest person,
answer all questions.

I might lie,
but remain unasked.

Detached, dangling
fetishized testicles.

My historical careless causality
of bated waiting frightens me,
fitting myself.

First name, middle name,
obsessing over withheld, hinted last:
truncated, common, Irish.

Flipping photos of curly dog,
chocolates of approval,
astounding endowment,
kayak at purple sunset,
cruiser remodeled on dock,
you in BMW sunglasses,
you goofing with girlfriend
on supermarket sculpture,
you offering assets to air.

Flipping stories of decrepit cat,
signed karaoke, iconic concerts,
prohibited phat dance crew videos,
shopping sassy with mother,
drinking Jäger with brother,
admiring hearing-aided athletes,

bed built unpainted pine
lingering in husband's house.

Dismantled,
but questioning correction
of emotional aftermath.
Squelching ache
for ideals of openness.

Are you on a date?

I could still care less.

Afraid tomorrow evening
is the Persian appointment.
I'll own assignation.
Set hot dads for some.

What's this tower, sweet?
Release our romance. I try,
but you sequester.

Waiting for offer,
spoiled against another.
Wake me with pet names.

Trick questions twang
somatic puppetry,
axons of thwarted desire.

Calling without words,
delay and cliché
engender furies of body.

Researching squirrels' screaming.

Staying my hand, holding
distance and successful Persian
standing biweeklies
over this hopeful head.

No significance:
penises in pool,
friendliness of Devon Rexes,
bathtub gin and incantations.

Grouped to watch vines grow,
grasping tendrils across walk,
up window screen, entwining
rows of unripe passion
toward their hot tub.

Craving resonance,
your texts making true
though urging on pitfalls
as bargain of parity.

The Persian looms, offering
his faultlessness to hips,
your panting neck kiss.
No platform for demands,
no raised eyebrow correction.

Insist I'm spinning myself,
baroque romantic tropes
nullified brusque.

Sweet yesses on sake,
welcome vulnerability.

You're probably passed out.

Chirp of night frogs
so dog and I step wary,
peering into misty shadows
shrouding suburbia.

Near where opossum once was,
flick phone to illuminate
shrieking baby bat
abandoned on pavement.

Curtained homes glow,
movement rare within.
Avert eyes, avoiding perversion.

Untold red flags,
Republican rally
of agonized anxiety.

Soundless,
notices words' rhythms,
memorizes meaningful lyrics,
believes I'm a prize.

I had hope.
I wriggle from no hope.

Your nervousness was cute.
Cowardice? Not cute.

Teen boy song sentimentality.
I can't prove anything he says.

Scrolling through mug shots
and search results,

failing to track down
traces of something true.

My buspirone stops sustaining.

Voices on repeat,
phrases of paranoia,
tapping at the Persian
like tongue on infected tooth.

Sick of being a little older,
a little wiser.

How much missing
is nonexistent?
Admonition flapping
into humidity,
steaming lies rippling.

Little hope, lot of effort,
sleepless nights radiating

purple lightning out chakras,
indicators of love based on
believable bullshit.

Or guarded soul,
curated identity,
deflected attention,
rich image consistencies,
sustained in-jokes, parceled
protected information doled
in certainty.

Sociopathic cruelty
necessary to torment
at this level of invention.
Citadel construction
with no edification.

Researched buzzwords
of what I would love.

Shocked my currency
of caring so common.

Clenched drive of courage,
plan by gymnasium fire door,
circuit YMCA locker room,
interrupt your leg exercises,
deflect strangers' advances,
force face-to-face at last.

Rehearsing hello, why
did you disappear,
withholding ghost?
Or ghosted extends
desire to suffer rebuff.

Silence expected: mute, deaf, shy—
bonds forged in intimate chitchat
overcome barriers, allow us existence.
Dismayed by plaintive pathos.

Worst probability you
won't resolve, this gym
breadcrumb location

invention, misdirection,
and you refuse to be.

Nothing to write home about,
compliments and strikeouts,
absent your handsomeness.

Aggrandizement demands approbation,
cycle inevitably to missing you,
searching solace in rounded biceps,
stretched tug across panoptic chest.

No heat to hug, embrace
devoid of undercurrent, another
buddy, another.

Setting dates with slapped-down
candles, but available instead
of isolated nursing insecurities.

I'd welcome you between heartbeats.

Fancy farmhouse with naked
circular driveway over culvert
in orange August afternoon.

This one had left, was late,
alarmed by bad news: mother
car wrecked, rushed to hospital
and taller than his pictures.

Thought to cancel, but need,
I already there in abandoned air.
Disrobed unsurprising, served
prepped purposes.

Exit interview washing bits
in sinks like raccoons.
Him: Will this happen again?

We can't know
how worlds will turn.

Forgot sunglasses inside,
so stopped at Sunoco
for replacement pair.

I'd marry you existentially.

Sexuality of Scorpio in water,
navigating islands of making believe.

Why summon phantasm,
fragmenting humiliation?
Taste disappointment,
quickening, test
I could still suffer.

Harshing Appomattox,
describing areas of absence
in keen deficiency.

Such Plain Jane pain, basic
bruised ego, desperate banquets,

waffle hopes. Your wringing
of fabric into ridiculous
but reflective shapes.

Bussing chapels
into neighborhoods
where they can't belong.

Psalm I meant to hear.

This one talks weather.

Summer's swampy hell mouth.
He loves summer.

I miss winter,
interiorizing intellectual retreat,
forced into basket weaving,
sharpening flints, surviving on nuts,
dried berries until spring.

Veneer of civilization diorama
detailing conformity, decision
of pretty safety in same vein.

Place fabricated, agreed
garden atop squelched swamp
with real fire ants in it.

Shrug, dismissive.

What gift to party,
whatever shall I wear.
Only smile.

Check inhibitions
at garden gate,
swimsuit in car.
Dizzy in bougainvillea's aroma.

Bones and body beautiful,
but tedium reconvenes
as combination ends.

Whom to touch departed early,
nobody left a friend.

Scarlet philter of figs,
rising heat allowed to smolder,
simulacrum of burn.

False contemptuous desire,
daring in silence.
Driving disappointed
with startling violence.

Praise reaches
comical proportions: girth
but not petit or grand—
folktale slides easily inside.

Enough challenge
to love flash of fear,
anticipation of pain
subsumed by beneficence.

That hits the spot.
Feel good, buddy?

Good enough,
flesh into form,
heated fricative,
generic satisfaction.

Pebbles and smallness,
mouse hero, tiny house
with miniscule furniture,
itty-bitty credenza, minute toilet,
infinitesimal flatware,
monstrous palmetto bugs
stomping shuddering halls.

Spindly serrated legs twitching
while rest of roach battles
house become sink,
tap gushes steaming

on bug struggles
to climb bubbling drain.

Sink walls too slick,
sink walls so sleek.

Macrocosmic, flinging
trajectory beyond universal turtle,
spinning outstretched fringes
into diffusion of matter,
scattering light, gravity in retreat,
you turned inside out.

Missing is lonely mystery:
omission perpetuating itself,
questions of lingering connection
twanging chords of empathy
to empower emotion
but directionless in intent.

I miss you. Platitude,
beginner's lesson on par
with toddler words of love.

Longing, because slow
takes taffy hours
worrying pulled tooth.

Shawled grim on widow's walk,
searching tide pools for personal
pattern of your cable knit sweater,
you're gone to sea.

Return to me.

I cannot absolve
your last confession.
I haven't the rite.

Order of deception
beyond reparation.

No sweet comedy,
romantic de Bergerac
duplicity revealing
kindred soulmate.

It is dripping horror.

You are the monster
who ate my man.

More fool, stories resurface,
narratives valued emblematic,
created from holy cloth and spit.

You never had lake house,
no Catalina day cruiser,
no cat Bartleby,
no dog Stanford,

no bubble butt intern,
no reason to cry gifted
with congratulatory chocolates.

No querulous family in Vegas,
no Midler's heroic "fly" in ASL karaoke,
no mother-beloved bears,
no hip hop crew on YouTube,
no horse head pornography,
no rescued roommate, no interpreter
or assistant shopper, no Berkeley,
or Walnut Creek childhood,
no industrial architecture,
or unpainted wood chaise
presented as wedding gift.

You never met Marlee Matlin
or cuddled Farrah Fawcett's lap.

No controlling husband beaten
by bent iPhone and estranged,

no adoption paperwork process,
no Persian ensconced above spa.

The knowing torments
inflicted with prevarication.

Let me study signing
in encouraged earnestness.

Nonchalance of gym times,
leg day, indoor swimming pools,
kayaking, concerts for the deaf,
Chinese top, trucker suck,
tech brother ne'er-do-well
joking about wifebeaters.

Nudes and smirks stolen,
intimidating physicality,
dozens of memorized textures
dissipating in humiliation haze.

Don't ever message me again.

I'll only get meaner from here.

Not merely catfished but gaslit,
disabusing fears with reassurances
to doubt dubiety, circumvent intuition,
dare to hope, begin to believe.

Who entertains Cassandra
with bespoke masculinity on offer?

Shallow rapaciousness of beauty,
solemn awe strictly taboo to filch,
fraud of greater currency,
power reiterating reward.

Beauty bounces, reflects scattered
particles of mercurial moonlight,
bathing fortune's few in radiance,
eclipsing else in blue vacuum.

He isn't you.

You cannot claim
stolen piecemeal charm,
suit of handsome skin,
disabled resilience earned.

That grotesque golem
undermines requisite truth.

This lap, then one more,
then swap strokes:
butterfly, dogpaddle, crawl.

Wavering NASA 1 overpass,
speed to be torn apart,
metal screeching as rent.
Bouncing off dividers, flipping
across lanes, tumbling battered,
dissociated screaming

surety of death, tossed
into safety glass shattered.

Instead drift, follow flow,
hang loose in monkey mind,
trust reflexes and signals,
pace with follower before
to sustain body in time.

This street again. This turn.
No changes in routine,
noticing what stretches ahead.

With nothing but what
I carry, what I've absorbed,
with gaps where
uncertainty was.

Debating deletion.
What will be handy,

what already uploaded
to the cloud.

Reflection unrecognized.
Portly penguin, hairy spaghetti
in dissatisfaction as canaries
fulfill wasted coal mine canards.

Creep along, fish for compliments,
and delve into darkest secrets,
divvy shame to pride,
clarify to hubris,
burned in brazier again.

On offer, not bargained
but a steal, fire sale
of blistered pictures
and charred books,
knowing smoky smell
won't diminish
from my loveseat.

What we have
is all we should give.

After

Supplies

Knocker of sticks and fruit,
calming spirit of unknown valleys,
taken analgesic with proprietary demands
on a salt shaker of tumbled wonderment.

Fowl and fluttering high in bursts
of squawking feathers, ancient
panicked Chinese ladies on the bus
freaked by indeterminate reroute.

The poetry upstairs, the pizza
around the corner. Groups
holding hands in swaying circles
and singing about sisterhood.

Questions extraneous
reflected in spectacles, beyond
easy reassurance and simple refund.

What slide, amber eyes, explains need,
consoles jealousy with admirable answers,
and does away with wayward water?

Drowning frog, flipped out,
instant insistence on return,
drawn to violence and instinctual
suicide in rippling blue.

This flicker, a partial request,
a generous bequest, offered
insight of glimmering mirage.

Appreciate the self-identification,
outdoor sconce semaphore, flashing
patterned warnings of hauntings, or
religious zealotry in strained homeschool.

The affiliations of hatred proudly
exhibited, lawn signs of liars,
furies but swallowed in tolerant
acquiescence to subordinate motion.

Swarms of mosquitos sucking blood,
stippling skin at every pause.
Sniff faster, my love, or we
will require transfusions this night,
with insufficient gin and tonics
to save us from diseases of grass.

Let's go, take the pill, relax
and the lilies unfold.

Just this piece, no other,
must be justified and redeemed,
while elsewhere weeds overtake the house.

Brood

Inconsiderate bird, stole seeds from needier
creatures and secreted in solitary nests
to selfishly supply a hoard unshared.

Disobedient fish, darting to hide in murk
what schooling imparted to social endeavor
but refused to use in community necessity.

Craven snake, coiled in damp coolness while
waiting for improvidence to pass and dismissed
family dangers as too exposing of oneself.

Egotistical frog, denying attempts to reconcile
misplaced eggs, refusing spawn responsibilities,
traveling free from the tethers of tadpoles.

Intemperate mouse, clinging to resentments
despite revelations of decent intentionality,
stewing over slights and gnawed vengeance.

Distracted grasshopper, leaping requirement to diversion where duration of effort is lesser but rewards never burgeon beyond minimal.

Lazy squirrel, sleeping away summers in haze of inertia over projected difficulty of extra endeavor and requiring relativity to sustain.

Gracious

for Sean

Alarming doctors and cute nurse
in his scrubs, alarming appointments
to be shrunk, to tutor language,
alarming to pick up prescriptions,
the bread is ready, the phone bill due,
this politician requests a pop up,
you just wanted to say hello, alarming
how long I'll wait for your next.

If I were a bit more babelicious,
would you break down my door?
If I text selective words of seduction,
will you repose against my pillows
in resplendent accommodation?
If I front the coolest kindness,
will you submit to dominating me?

When do you sleep? I was
nocturnal too, before dog.

Outreach by a verifiable
new person in the world.

Trickster with the long ears, I promise
golden carrots, first born daughters,
a lost lamb in the maze of hedgerows,
a tearing of my raveled weft.

Expected refusal, demurral, nope,
lost and sundered until
the coming coalesce.

Fingered twelve and the loss
was a blow to the head but
least important insults us all
no matter how we transcend the flesh.

Friended in haste but permanently cemented,
a wish for groupings and circles,
a need for peeps who ride your back,
tires screeching in the sheeting rain,
hydroplaning through unsafe puddles.

A paucity of new nouns, unused verbs,
stuff unfamiliar and untried, tired
and wild, birds landing unidentified
on the banister, tilting their jerky heads
in clinical curiosity and offerings of alms.

Snap the pattern, realigned wheel of stars,
ask a pauper how he is to survive
and plan accordingly, by new rules,
in acknowledgment of future supernovas.

You're sexy like gravity, a theorem
of universal applicability,
payment rendered in chattel or kind.

Plead for a freebie, a present wrapped
in silver foil, reflecting an open eye,
while forgotten names worry and wander,
ever sounding incorrect and off.

Break this encroached standard,
bust an edifice of warping woods,
and strike out into an unknown
where the words await invention.

This wasn't what I wanted,
but you were a discovery, unasked,
ineluctable, frightening, and shimmering
with a faithless need beyond hope.

That flagpole and texture, the burgers
and niece sadness, agree it's unfair
but we all have pain, nobody is good
enough, we don't remember the divine
connection that animates us all,
and we bruise like dropped nectarines.

I never asked for the images,
the circular repetition of incremental
grins and crinkly eyes and pitted cheeks,
overrule a cap of black hair,
that snagging bristle of fur,
and exquisite softness in my hand.

Laurel

What hasn't initiated in randomness,
or developed structure in the afterglow,
when specific thematic avenues are
required to focus attention in order
to be followed in shared narrative
and admired by the bronzed spoons?

Do we ever inherently, unerringly understand
the impurities of which we speak,
or do the impact electricals overwhelm
the imperative of coherent expression,
or the keys clatter in concentrated
ecstasy, fallen anarchy, urged urgency,
rushed and desperate obsession in attempts
to renew the avenues of approbation?

Declarative exhaustion, released fever,
a fervor of overweening self-creation

extols accomplishments of past iteration,
apologizes for the gushes of exhortative
compliments and intangible obfuscations,
no faster reinvented then collapsed in
blackbird pie counting-house contradiction.

A rhetoricized consistency was never
wanted, unwarranted and weak,
so the chimes of initiation sound
and hope opens the code and interprets again.

Rides of the patient, elongated
elephants stepping stately among the stones,
dangling pendulous ovoids in the void,
gathered to bear the brunt of fatherhood.

A cut across a fingertip, echoing
tales of overindulgent sociality,
scarred purple by unnecessary parties
to which invitations were reluctantly offered
and too desperately accepted before-thought.

I feed your face, your minimum outlay
of subdued energy, your cling to
surprisingly warm and puttered pleasure.

All play and no work, more dramedy,
innocent laughers coughing
to hide amusement in danger park.

Lost in infinite reflections, shattered
eternity in dark warped ripples
and framed, one-sided assertions.

It's better without this battered
and bruised return to the familiar
when the wheel won't rotate that way.

One piece to represent all,
one golden tether to the infinite
especially unknown by those who know.

Western

A cat, a horse, a carriage
ridden away by a midnight thief,
the bounty never claimed,
a posse unformed.

Shrugged stolen moments,
pilfered hearts cease to beat,
and the owner lay in the road,
arms protecting his skull from harm.

Wanted and dusty, bereft,
a stranger moseys in, chickens
aflight, and the schoolteacher
swoons in his patched gabardine.

A saloon, a spittoon, at low noon,
and the golden hearts swing
from the tinkling chandeliers
as ivories clatter flat distractions.

Watchmen dream in boots,
whistling under shelter of a Stetson,
and our sheriff locks the doors,
key in his pants, barred until daybreak,
when the prospector's ghost leaves
his lost lover and hides in mine.

Nothing

for Jeff

Sheets creep along Blomidon beach
and claw furrows as hermit crabs celebrate
conjugation to grasp fingertips turned blue,
finding purchase on glistening sea glass.

Accentuated sex but rooster crowed,
haphazardly anarchic, chaotic, slapdash,
punctuating consistent hunt, however
unsuccessful in duel procurement.

Cliff crumbles into cracker dusting
and streamers squiggle away untrustworthy
so the mud prints filled in gleaming scent
along the flats sucking at our hiking boots.

Tides enormous ferried and fraught,
winds shorten creeping heather leeward

to pick a goat path on the buffeted stone
promising comfortable currency.

Extended inaugural pride of coupling,
breakfast teamwork, alcohol scowls, mapping
ambushed trails, reciting tints of green.

Detonated ship blasted the Halifax harbor,
a searing flash necessitating glass eyeballs
and a specific tool for original removal,
encased in a glinting museum room.

Sleep fights in kicks and snores
though the day road didn't disapprove.
Not kind but unexpected helpfulness
upended treed hills and sought old hosts.

The priest's window ghost winked at us,
graves umbrellaed out from summer's find,
and eye-blue skies chilled the cobblestones
when you mumbled love as I went home.

Iterate

Comprehension approaches in argument
to blank nearness of a chirping alarm
unheard in familiar debated silence
given low marks in mechanical lead.

The muscle of thought, of retaining
tweaks a redoubtable record of need
and casts accomplishment in harsh appraisal
while dry tongue jokes in flat affect.

Break a compilation of honor and pity,
the fussy table a foreign arrangement,
discomfiture leaning near the margin
but ants in letters scurry their clues.

The dollar isn't even a minute,
respectfully bowing nose to the carpet,

while research falters in false generals
and memory hatches parrots of prey.

Dangling participle, I perfected the past,
had run the laps with flapping laces,
how wrong were the words of invitation
corrected by divine madness understated.

An awkward handshake, an offer unrealized,
incoming projections of business horizons
and tempers lost as time fidgets
which traveled expenses can't unbind.

Not for nobody, the tongues of flame,
but greatest desires differentiate the similar,
and oligarchical hegemony breaks the future
to a preacher proclaiming the agreeable.

A union, a drone, a hive of honey
needs fortune to lessen the moaning.

Alternate information injures our overlay
and fearfully aggravates tumescence.

I'm available in time, expecting a nod
of recognition, a realization furrowed
by rakes with unholy intentions awakening
misconceived terrors of forsaken lords.

Do not demand obedience to beliefs
when falsehoods increase and accumulate
in populated exponents hating all others
unbothered to acknowledge intimidation.

Insulated by thievery, shielded by weaponry,
clinging to traditions desperately aging,
look to the loser for sustenance and mercy
and ignore the safe havens that accustom us.

Not a nostalgia for past patterns of behavior
or a rewriting of standards of extreme avoidance

finds an excuse to put off necessity's focus
when concentration is the costliest of forces.

The swiveling chair, eyes bleary from nearness,
the sizes of mountains teetering skyward
can demotivate the laborer with blistered wrists
and children who require designer sneakers.

Stand firmer on response, abient desire,
skip cooking or clothing or afternoon napping.
Is it lazy or dreamy to await inspiration
as the years pass with minor triumphs?

Unactualized adulthood, admitted pathos,
a finite countenance of finished projections
and withered ambition awaited to foment
a rush of activity to bolster the present.

Words without anchors or trustworthy simile,
no objects to represent a greater ad hominem,

a lamppost seen across the fenced yards
while the garden remains in darkness.

A miswrought conclusion, altered facts,
and all attempts trickle like salt.

We cannot find the full range of grace
until all the interlaced is accepted.

Hike

Shutter the shut up, Mary, divide the prize.

Follow suspicions in night vision past shrubs.

Lock the windows, get the rifle, call 911.

Ominous footsteps, flickering neon, nobody.

Paid the vig and placated this visit.

Cakes in Germany rising to glowing birthday.

Achieved a push through but stairs.

Plowed a roadblock and widened defenses.

This rat, that skunk, kicked to the curb.

All papers in, the work filed and forgotten.

Cotton sinuses excusing from the table.

Ignored triumph knew a rationalization.

That stick is too big, that tree too tall.

Break a leg, dearest, someday

can't help vibrating the same pain.

Merge

The story is whittled away
until only traditional rituals remain.

Splattering rain pocks the concrete,
eroding the edifices of mercy.

Clouds of infinitesimal winged creatures
haze the air but remain unfelt, parting
in shyness or perhaps too insubstantial
to affect the sensors of the skin.

The capless acorns roll underfoot,
wobble and skid oblong marbles,
treacherous as windmills.

A rough patch, a ragged nail,
dead pine needles fusing to rusty goo,
extra unexplained sand in the folds,
and broken clamshells sixty miles inland.

Repeat again, season by season,
into standards and codified, crystallized
directives that brook no argument
because they've no reply in the morning.

Repeat to gather energy and family,
chant and rhyme to reconvince,
and the stars grow brighter
until we cannot separate our blink
from distant radiation across the dark.

Nineteen

for Adam

He's sorry for his sorrow,
banging the marrow of swollen bones,
pushing taut thighs of excuses,
toil and redouble troubled humor.

Tired thrusts of minimal frisson
focus on tightness thwarting connection,
embracing a heated curve of camaraderie,
protests countered with skillful assurances.

Hoarder of hobbies divorced a preacher
whose queer spirit hung unreleased.
The devil is messy, too, returns at dawn,
dismayed at finding corridors of refuse.

A home beached in tourist trade
comforts kitchens declared forbidden,

and critters burrow in mammalian dens
but lose reunions in strains of age.

Questioned lies left to lay requested,
skin sheathed prevents unequal trusting.
Fauns fawning over satirical satyrs
diminish a moment of possible pleasure.

Meaning disported but offhand, slowly,
find a favored spot in uneasy fervencies
and release youth in fine recumbent form
to find a peaceful idyll of quiescent fleece.

Seizure

It will be told the rivers
shall swell with rust and vermin
through underground tunnels straining
to bear the solvent waters
and lessen in familiar grace.

Over bones a cycle of weeds
yellow flowers and pollen collectors
grand as inflated hippopotamuses
buzz spiky fields undulating with worms.

The birds flightless again, striding
to peck and flap at outsized insects,
pull each other apart in screeching
that signals how unsafe the night.

Where are we? Out on the salty
oceans, on pontoon islands, canoes

and yachts hooked together to surf
the storms, ricocheting
from uninhabitable coast
to toxic beach, following
the angry, fluctuating jetstream,
chanting prayers to sea gods
into the boiling morning sun.

We are already adapting,
salty babies crawling along ropes
and gangplanks, befriending the sea
mammals, adjusting to a diet of kelp
and krill, telling terrifying stories
of the glass canyons of man,
the creeping poison of our mistrust
and the flood promised never to return.

Power has reverted to matriarchy,
sea witches healing and midwifing
and auguring the weather,
influencing the direction

of the wind and breeding
of family stock.

Gestation slowed to incubate
to specification, but redundancy
foments scorn by generation, compliances
of drones, peaceful as rainwater brooks
but quieter, less tendency to overrun.

Codified standards of fact, policies
and amendments to truth decided
by representational committees of stern
traditionalists and calcified academics,
quick checklists of honesty,
no lies but narrow avenues
of ambiguity rarely allowed.

Religions dampened to outlaw sects,
sex projected in few combinations,
physical pleasure matter-of-fact as eating was.

A certain safety valve of rebellion
and expression allowed to churn
in certain submerged centers,
children with talent and anger
separated and inserted into enclaves
of opposition and artistic endeavor,
factories of entertainment and inspiration,
enough to kindle a reduced vanguard
of progression, as an unevolving
organism is soon extinct.

Those with scientific aptitude
are similarly sequestered on buoys,
given education and equipment to stir
the advancement of invention,
but without fame or privatization,
destructive impulses culled
for the safety of the sphere, for
common interest, with corruption
delegated to the accused accursed.

What engenders improvement, motivates
competition, enlivens ambition,
those forces of humanity that must
be addressed before they curdle into
dissatisfaction, languor, insurrection,
how to manifest incentive when
everyone has equal discomfort and
access to their destined birthright.
Why do we get up in the morning,
what urges us to come and try,
what justifies and gives purpose to life.
Why strive in a system of oppressive
yet comfortable equality afloat.

No fairy tale significance to opiate
and distract from suffering, no
chemical solace of serotonin uptake,
so what brings meaning to the passage
of time in its tedious but brief floating span.

Is it a lottery of love, a bribe
of romance, or simply a satisfaction

of achievement in an existence
provided with plenty but grinding
the many under a yoke of work
and mental oppression at sea.

We finally harnessed our strangest
intrinsic attribute, and elevated altruism
to fetishized pledged mottos of intent.

Dogs, cats, rats are with us,
roaches and beetles, spiders
and lizards, sea lions, and octopuses
clinging to the trailing lines like
waterskiers, twirling in kaleidoscope
colors to obscure the edges of our ecosystem.

The land is salted, bracken, blistered,
and although the grass grows ever taller,
it belongs to the birds, bees, and worms.

Closer

The witch watches from the pool,
his false green eyes intent on petting,
thick thighs dimpled and unflattering,
requesting rides from distant schools.

A gang of lost keys, black smiles,
drunken wandering and begging aid,
aggressive backing up, impaling
and taken by turns of angry thrust.

We all were drugged by choice,
with warnings; accusations of impropriety
puerile but understandable given
self-protective shame rationalized externally.

Everyone was young once.

Unfun, even grim, these orgiastic impulses,
the escapades presented regularly sought

or unexpected but consistently wayward
on the outskirts of what may be expressed.

It's my birthday, take these off,
why the resistance to a certain want.
Exchanging bathing suits on the beach,
an urge relinquished to abashed loyalty.

Apologize in the bubbling hot tub,
accepting rubs as reimbursement.

The regrets I've pondered upon
are seldom for an intemperate push,
but for fearful prospects squandered.

Omen

Anxious creature, screaming in hugs.

Muggy strides under hazy gibbous glow.

The long cross, the tug and hurry.

Worried applicants in alternated directions.

Infected with terrors, inspected by insurance.

Reassured by rationalized leaps of confidence.

Dense destiny waits, unreached and patient.

Fainted reclinations feigned of action.

Attraction unnecessary for required tasking.

Masked aggression, faith not for troubles.

Leaning closer so servers passage.

Mass delusion enacted in triumphant legislation.

Regulated emotion detailing distant interest.

Finish the playbook, indomitable power.

Scratch

Maintaining certitude despite no recognition,
applying again in peaceful progression,
unconsidered insult, unappreciated but
positive about the animating powers of intent.

The dragonflies swoop and hover, darting
above the rusty marsh, iridescent carapace
catching the sunlight and insect attention.
Cling to the flower, prey on mosquitos,
and never concerned with correctness.

The bundled landscapes look at us,
walking dog on suburban sidewalks,
eyes askance and unreadable. We
live our challenges and rewards,
or discomforts and triumphs,
but depressed and unearned privilege
cannot be wished away.

Pick a topic, a noun of metaphoric value,
a flower, purple twining morning glory,
and relinquish control to the overgrowth
choking out life in a vined embrace.

Taking another break, a nap in a car,
a nap in the pool, a nap in the park,
shirking duty or exhausted after focus,
a vow of never enough tempers expectations.

The mushrooms hump and parasol,
grotesque fleshy protuberances of
vigorous decay, vegetative but ungreen,
entangled and symbiotic, toxic spored,
blemishing and rotting the rapture of lawn.

Relying on animal enthusiasm, tethered
to the pull, leashed to obsession,
the wellspring gushes down the funnel,
and we step through the shadows but still
break a sweat in the cool of evening.

The brilliant scarlet and hot fuchsia
won't sustain reproductive reflection
and where the hot whiteness hits
overexposure sharpens in ugly bleach.

Purples, yellows, browns hold in rainy
overcast, but merely contrasted, dull
without the dancing interplay of sunlight
forcing seared translucence on petals.

Cropped for drama, straightened for
formalism, the clarity is rarely adequate,
and seek the moment when magic
clicks in the synchronicity of clockwork.

The stink of concentration is unclean,
but reeks of satisfied accomplishment
even as dizziness demands recumbence
to recover again in pampered rest.

Hard

Coherency of form doesn't matter,
although hardness is a property of import.
I press the screen lightly so it doesn't crack
another broken crown afraid to afford.

The cakes and folding chairs are stacked
but you've vanished into vagaries of fiction.
I can't attract with these unfair comparisons
the spouse of pardon who chooses to laugh.

Chat and expand a date into two
but scuttle the intro to avoid exhaustion
and spend precious hours flirting again
with he who has two husbands at home.

A second marriage, left a woman for a man,
broken sexual distance unworthy to follow,
opening time but allowing no agenda
and still returning to fish the same ice.

Seeking epic happiness leaves me sadder,
silvered, chunky in tedious sexual ennui.
Swum poundage removed but ever heavier
while suffocating for possibility to surface.

Shelter

The hallway stretches and amazes
through metal stacks along carpeted paths,
unidentified paintings on the walls
between check out rooms, student powwows,
and lunches spread around glowing laptops.

I follow my worn trail of feet
along a repetitive route, considered
adjusting but the rapture of the regular
compels familiar direction and pace.

The failures of liberalism, truth about mice,
German audio books and identical spines
of dissertations presumably forever unread.

The shared offices of personnel, the chairs
empty along extra-formal desks avoiding
stares, head on high, no ownership
but allowed and welcomed nonetheless.

Find a favorite carrel, one empty without
exposed screen to aid procrastination,
the setup, the audio antennae alert
for sounds of chewing or plastic wrap.

What does my silver signify
to the students, is it unnoticed
or unimportant, and I recognized
and identified, or outro, ignored?

It's possible that experience
is the currency of the afterlife.

Which aspect matters more,
the wasteland wind howling like wolves,
or the desktop clutter of sentimental value,
a question coughed into tissue and wiped
clotted before irritation turned to concern.

Patterned hoodie comforts agreeably offered,
named once, twice, and then misremembered
to devalue substance over general acceptance.

Close enough is not good enough, read
the directions, follow the instructions,
check the address before purchase,
or don't complain when the bursar rebills.

Distracted by missing digits, forgotten button,
missed loops and lost teeth from sweets,
an adopted tragedy in furry grumbles,
spotting blood with aged pain again.

Leaching color, tone, strength, clarity,
where photographic editing reveals
the shame of decomposition and
withers the confident youth in time.

Hide me in here, this bright cavern,
while the history of us whispers urges
to offer my updates to the transcript.

Bandy

Piglet faultline, anonymous donor
question mockery, growl meekly
afraid of mice, toothless forgiven
quarter to two, alligator in bayou rising

Smelt the ring, quilting bee now
killing time, satsumas on the lawn
dawning glory, knots upon knots tied

Don't lie, the confessor knows our face
pick-up sticks, furtive glances in shop
sweltering pedal, mirror gray distance
glutes perked, scowl to define

Tricked again, a train tunneling
rumble worries, rattletrap quarantine
compare scars, transfer into starry night

Grumble fur, losing mass to teeth
blunt cut, tired but caring

paid bills, accounting whereabouts
found hope, summon coping soon

Watched pot, knives in dishwasher
touch lamp, eyes hooded and mean
quality row, noon free of swollen fears

Bronzed

Calling forth the guardians of virtue
to reconcile the retconned choices
of anger, laziness, and petty petulance
crowds sleep like a beanie of bees.

Elevate the heels, wriggle the thighs,
fearing the brownout of attention
lost in fogs of overcast skies.

A few more steps, mind the gap
as the platform regulates at dusk,
bruises of unknown origin and platters
of nuggets panned from a parted river.

Unconsidered explanations of criminality
surface, slippery, dismaying our agreements,
and clatter like hail on a plastic porch.

Mosquitos drone, unflushed gurgled hiss,
we wait for silence to reassert,

still the ripples that warp focus
and frame the blur into comprehension.

The words must mean something,
for how can language be meaningless,
to what end the synaptic connection
of lily pad and pumpkin carriage?

The chirp of night frogs communicates
without connotation, and felines startle
by insinuating language is unnecessary
to thrive, that life interacts anyway
no matter the false firework display
taken as a celebration of victory
over ships and flags and floating bodies
among crates of caffeine and taxation.

Every story has a disclaimer, a step
beyond the facts of twisted relevance.
The mother hoarded dreams to counter
depression of inertia, the father
was not the soul he bought at cost.

Our child grew awry, hated to look
us in the eyes, desperate to disavow.

Tell me again the recipe, the items
that must be collected from sources
in places we never imagined could be
reached, explored, adapted, and
forgotten so that the particulars repeat.

Armaments aplenty, take refuge in now,
drive carefully the leaping sheep,
and slumber in pastures of not yet.

Drift

Sick as the clock shakes hands
brittle under my nightcap of crickets
fallen into patterns regrettable,
grasping at days' dwindle.

Unfixable, monstrous recognition
found anew in the still marsh
and yet unsurprising, familiar,
asleep in the mirroring meadow.

Afraid again of nonrecombinance,
affected by avowed origin,
weirdling ceremonies around stew
spiced with dreaming and courage.

Asking ages to determine presence,
minded impertinence in locale,
stutter-stepping into qualitativity,
purchasing friendliness in open air.

Forget the dance steps of unplanning,
awaken again to daily diminution,
ducking correction, neglect a groom,
and explain the joke to drain its juice.

Tired plays stomp the floodlights
as dust disseminates to reseed welcome.

Best

for David

Lean in, Eiffel and meld, Jacob's ladder
voltage arc in pink connection, empathy
hurtling over corporeal hurdles to avow
acknowledgement of communal smarts.

Mockery over the texture of terra cotta,
department fabrics, sticky sidewalk scores,
tree toads on bewigged bunny lane,
dancing seven veils, fowl laying eggs
in sped-up revolutions per minute.

Choosing a personal fragrance as
a signature of lingering attraction—
rubbed wrists of red reaction, sniffed
white candles of bitter flowers and Orangina.

Pay for good hair, for purses flying out,
a view of the private pool and mountains.

Brushes of bronze, masks of earth,
and muds and waxes to coif the quiff.

Bunting woven on the banisters, draped
blue and white behind matrimonial balloons,
entwined around trees and horneted planters,
dogs and children in ties under the stairs.

Make me laugh again, my friend,
dispel dark storms with airy silliness,
squawk stinky indignation and judgment,
and bull's-eye pin-point references
to jump in a lake to retrieve the dead bird.

Hold him burning, scorched by iron,
variegated by vitiligo and poshness,
the murdered Jetta, the music of rocky
roads, and rage at the flannel pickup trucks
driving too poky to get to bloody brunch.

Motion

Gasps of perfume and popcorn surround
awkward arms and plastic wrap crinkling
waiting for the main event, the return
to continuum, multiverses defying vacuum.

The quiet creep of fingers inching into gummy
recesses of nuts and bolts and used tissue
climbing the ironworks, passing padding
to feel for the current of tactile vitality.

Damp and ridged, distanced and oblique,
eyes fixed focus on subliminal flashing
to excuse the conscience from forgiveness,
supplying plausible deniability to the flesh.

Fumble protected in darkness, heightened
awareness of potential sightlines, shadows,
silhouettes informing others of broken codes
of turpitude, signals of succumbing to cliché.

The fits and frets of loneliness forgotten
in the motion of meanwhile and accepted
coincidences recognized as progression
of proper fate while cringing at impropriety.

Loosen shoulders, slump into acquiescence
as unfolding illumination streaks across
molecules and ripples of etheric quintessence
to splash vividly colored stories on concurrency.

Exurb

Unsnapped synapses, distancing distraction
unseated kings and scuttled schooners, slumped
inebriated on splattered garret floorboards
and drifted south on sweetest greasy smoke.

Pinpointed willpower, wincing coughing masses,
tedium in scales and lessons of diplomacy
suffered drones and humming heat
while waiting to return to phantasmagoria.

A bit of a jolt, libido's satisfaction,
relief of fetishism in looping legs,
gust of freedom out of miasmic desire,
allowing crystal sight to descend.

Rearview of constancy, a struggle on tables
and clippings of political news, diagrams
of grasshopper segments and antennae
urged outward in hopeful lines.

The obsessions of interest, set aside
for the requirements of registration,
neglected to wither in palm fronds
and chewed tips of clip-on ties.

Released recrimination, trembling trees
along jagged faults crumbling concrete
and incorrect directions blindly grasping
for a miracle of electrical connection.

Neglected desire, these grasses submerged,
reflected bare cypress in concentric ripples,
frogs and night herons crying in cut reeds.

Thwarted ambition, shadows of clouds
on a hot summer hillside, rolling in fevered
hazes of pollen and shivering gamesmanship.

Familial resignation, wavering blue pool
crystalline with antiseptic chlorine, balanced
alkaline impurities tested by carcinogenic
conservatives who asked awkward questions.

Mortified status, disappointed by hyped storms
and floods becoming breezes and puddles
ruining medians of lawn but otherwise
uninterruptive in imaginative scope.

Effortless glibness, heightening sunset saturation
and contrasted to shock with cherry icicles,
stolen importance from more subtle sky.

Defied expectation, strolling through parks
along a tautened tether, far but no further,
patrolling sidewalks for unfounded inspiration.

Accepted insipidity, crossing the carpet
striped with footsteps repeated into trail,
extended trials of unused fortitude.

Conflagration of unhappiness, stolen
bitter twist from a punning uncle's story,
a lost lover who knew avenues of approach,
tied to sunrise fence posts disassociating pain.

Washing the screens, mud and bugs, scraped
claws against the mesh, tinny screech, flinched
at life and its jumping motion toward today,
movements synchronized in stellar orbs of ice.

Quit bitching, who cared who went first,
cried of parity and personality defections,
brave races of older horses on tracks of dust,
bet on the loser who located a mislaid locket.

Tried and bettered, passages of fault,
refused the glaring daggers of ocular insistence,
denied fears of miscommunication to touch
knowing, pushed the credible potential
to either exit to test alternatives of escape.

Expectations frayed, cried neighborly alarms
warn barking dogs, desired allotted aspiration,
and watched in slow shock past came to pass.

Sophist

Prickling at positivity, bristling at insistence
outlook influences experience in all directions,
as choice is less comprehensive than imagined
and masses in wretchedness would disagree.

Perhaps optimism only impacts events when
all concerns of survival have been satisfied.
Maybe starvation is a decision of desert people
subjugated by tribal dictators out of want.

Yes, the wave particulates when we peek,
yes, subjective desire influences the observed,
yes, refusal to whine reaffirms fervent vows,
yes, accentuating the positive is Marketing 101.

Life, though, cannot manifest only butterflies
or rainbows, no matter our attitude of approach.
Hope is not a consideration of the cosmic
clockwork, our fears do not gape the abyss.

Cellular rebellion, agony of the eaten, failure
to hatch, testing mettle do not necessitate
good feeling for avoidance or conquest.
The external patterns of chaotic snow remain
in unheeding existence, wasting as they will,
storming vicissitudes of improvidence.

Acceptance isn't influence; the drama unfolds
around and within us, the wind tears us from
the swaying elms no matter how we cling.

Our sincere prayer is not the only sound,
and singular will has no ascendancy over all.

Privy

Magnified mirror, suicide pores and hairs
journey into reflected reversals and oppose
expectation with fingers against cold glass.

Sonic vibrations of liquid bristles and sharp
pains of false porcelain veneer and pricey
spat pink, grinning with stains of scraped tea.

The lines of experience crease and fold,
improved expressionless, framed by whiteness
ever receding into ignorance despite desire.

Naked disappointment, familiar for despair
but steady in weathering inconfidence,
wryly amused condescension of aging appeal.

Who could love this ruined and bumpy hole,
this awkward organ of pleasure never expected
to require beauty that no ointment can heal.

Hog's body, horse's ass, goat face, doe eyes,
when attraction remains out of reason,
unquestioned for the pellets and eggs.

The whyfors of love circle useless as destiny
shapes its capricious occurrences and waits
for renewed hopes to burn in rising sun.

Knoll

for Samir

Epochal approach from beyond the ferns
surrounded by an umbra of lost time
and dreaminess, subsumed, summoned
to the court of the prince of silent secrets.

Statuesque, stately, fearsome, with eyes
of olivine, mesomorphic and precise,
a geologic being virile and nonvolatile
as the mantle requires sturdy obduracy.

Mannered cold, alone in a manor of marble
carved from metamorphic calcite in veins
that ceased to bleed in eons past.

Dining on roots and insect pastes,
obscured by company in solid stability,
he will never feign to love, heart valves

shut to thump, but all elements are lonely,
all atoms ache to interconnect.

Uncertain when the need to breathe
entered dormancy, when food faded,
when seconds lengthened into always,
and our borders fused in communion.

Dream of the taken, reach for him again,
and rest in the constancy of stone.

Gifts

No time serves like this convergent present
to unwrap traditional nostalgia in pretty bows,
intake furtive tinsel filaments, ornament hooks,
dismantle peace in tacks and irritated stoked soot,
worming too-familiar familial finger through
stocking hole to lose scratch lottery ticket, yellow
yo-yo, tremolo mouth organ, cunning token
of puzzle plastic, or an escaped cloven orange
delivered from distant Florida's sunny groves.

Pyramidal evergreen emblem of fountainhead,
connective nexus of received divinity, approving
primordial grace eternally uncertain of propriety
to exhibit twinkling trinkets of Saint Nicholas.

Precocious sugarpear fairy visions inducing
a sleepless overnight, acutely intoxicated panic
for dawn of cornucopian rapacious avarice
and cocoa marshmallow memories quietly

complicating bonds of semiannual community,
drowsy pleasures of giver's achieved surprise
mellowing in sated carols of angelic pageantry.

Holy appealing host, bodied and bloody,
donate alms of atonement or forgiveness,
epiclesis bestowing deliverance and desire,
pledge of cultural diplomacy, a bequest
of services rendered from a prostitute's
splurge from endowment, largesse intended
by benevolent bribes aiding oblation in kind.

Gift must remain greater than receipt,
even if covetousness circumvents our altruism,
crosses survival, and insists on a final thrift.

A shower to show him a gesture of gelt,
overgenerous eidi, chocolate rabbits eaten
ears first, blanching at manipulative reward
for abundant compliance, annual rebirth caked,
candled, and sung of sweetly ticking unease.

Pair parted, purple orchid pre-potted,
warmed a house scoped of thoughtfulness,
impressed with bleached fox skull, bluest
quilted bee, awkward emerald, chinchilla
stole as fresh and dirty favor, a begged bonus
of hastily borrowed prize oxen for nuptial
coronation, dinging a single golden doorbell,
donning wrist straps of fragrant surging corsage.

Cardboard anniversary, year of mildew and mold,
pewter jubilee with trussed mayflower tadpole,
commemorating again engagement of gregarious
telethon aligned to pious charity solicits solidarity
with brokered union assistance, undisclosed sums
of tax aversion, strict adherence to catalog lists,
requests, and registry wishes of white elephants
regifted to forestall burdensome deadweight loss.

What knickknack could you contribute, Daddy?
T-shirt travelogue, spoon and penny souvenirs
for critical accumulation from tragic zoo, football

dome, mustard museum, obtaining omiyage,
keepsake pasalubong to snuggle plush stuffed
representations, material ephemeral memorabilia,
bagged swag popcorn promotion, macaroons,
a ham, smuggled cheese, clever sour cherry jam,
drunk on personalized half pints of wine shipped
separately from outlying lovely, lonely vineyards.

Treat to a guilty boon of sinful goodies,
replacing literature of his whose library was
arsoned to ashes and smoldering coal.
Ouroboran ophidian of foreknowledge,
spark supplier, we shame and are ashamed,
ate fruit of decadent self-consciousness,
violating the vengeful oldster's orchard,
accepting an instructor's poisoned apple
to illuminate our awareness of immortality.

Our ordinary abilities enumerated and tested
in infancy, patterned against genetic destiny,
only nine lords annealing claimed attributes,
blamed deficiencies on the opposite aisle.

The rarest qualities jockey for ascendency:
lyric coloratura, hyperthymesia, tetrachromacy,
mathematic theorization of temporal dislocation,
culled clairvoyance, minute silicon synesthesia,
xenolalia, spontaneous kindness, dance ordered
angularity in slippery trinity on triangular tiptoe.

Embrace the scratched, seeping wellsprings of
creative composition, astounded by prodigiously
perfected mathematic musicality, trace back
source to inscrutable cosmic aquifer and despair.

Wiser men premised hopes on their promise,
followed glimmering wisps into murky woods,
wandered as polestars across dark desert voids,
pursued presumptuous question into dragon's lair
to land an intimate princeling hand and foot.

Alight pyrrhic incense, anoint rare myrrh,
and kowtow in gratitude to the shared object
of our tangible offering, incestuous sacrifices

slaughtered on hilltops, blood spilling scarlet
down worried steps, relics of offhand affection
signifying apology, stoical solitary acceptance,
and integrated exchange of converted energy
as requisite expression of our beloved devotion.

Coast

Amazing strange the spume of a moment,
the path through fate, driving on purpose
toward the event du jour, whatever's on offer,
paltry or magnificent in surprising scope.

Accepting invitations delivered by seagull,
deciding on dress, gift, attitude, interest
depending on the importance of personae
populating the gathering of shimmering waves.

Undersea is too easy, a foreign domain
with no ambassadors or visas or oxygen.
Might as well camp on the moon, we
are unmarked for oceanic ambitions.

Yet the scent, the rush and splash
and subsumed withdrawal pull at ankles,
suck into the purple-streaked sand,
a gasp of a partially substantiated ghost.

No party unfolds the same letter, no
conversation travels to the same shore.
The bottle sloshes with amber alcohol,
a warm burr that encourages friends.

In each minute we melt again, lost
through the hourglass, surfing a curl
of least resistance, drawing patterns
in the accretions and eddies of mist.

About the Author

Gene Hult was born on November 12, 1969 in New York City.

He has written more than 120 books published for children and young adults, mostly under his pseudonym J. E. Bright.

Gene was the Managing Editor of the literary journal *Denver Quarterly*. He then worked in children's publishing for more than 20 years, at houses including HarperCollins, Scholastic, and Simon & Schuster, until he left as an Executive Editor to write full-time.

Since 2017, Gene has lived with his dog Henry in the suburbs south of Houston, Texas, where he is a writer, editor, publisher, and teacher.

For more information, please visit **genehult.com** and **jebright.com**.

Brighten Press

The Power of Words to Enlighten and Entertain

With all the many other demands on your attention in the world, we appreciate you taking the time to read this book.

We welcome you to explore our growing list of poetry, humor, and children's book titles at **brightenpress.com**.

www.ingramcontent.com/pod-product-compliance
Lightning Source LLC
Chambersburg PA
CBHW060458080526
44584CB00015B/1472